OCRACOKE LIGHTHOUSE

Researched and Compiled
by
Ellen Fulcher Cloud

ISLAND HISTORY

Volume I. Ocracoke Lighthouse.

Other titles in preparation.

Ocracoke Lighthouse

Researched and Compiled
by

Ellen Fulcher Cloud

Published in Association with
LIVE OAK PUBLICATIONS
Ocracoke, North Carolina
by

THE REPRINT COMPANY, PUBLISHERS
Spartanburg, South Carolina
1993

An original publication, 1993
The Reprint Company, Publishers
Spartanburg, South Carolina 29304

ISBN 0-87152-471-6
Library of Congress Catalog Card Number 93-23759
Manufactured in the United States of America

The paper used in this publication meets the requirements of American National Standard for Information Sciences—Permanence of Paper for Printed Library Materials, ANSI Z39.48-1984.

Library of Congress Cataloging-in-Publication Data

Cloud, Ellen Fulcher.
Ocracoke Lighthouse / researched and compiled by Ellen Fulcher Cloud.
p. cm. — (Island history ; 1)
"Published in association with Live Oak Publications, Ocracoke, North Carolina."
Includes bibliographical references (p.) and index.
ISBN 0-87152-471-6 (alk. paper)
1. Ocracoke Lighthouse (N.C.)—History. I. Title. II. Series.
VK 1025.O27C57 1993
387.1'55—dc20 93-23759
CIP

To
Sally Newell
and
Kevin Cutler
for their help
in saving the windows
of
Ocracoke Lighthouse

Table of Contents

Photos and Illustrations

PREFACE

I was born and reared on Ocracoke Island, and, like most other Ocracokers, have thought little about the history of Ocracoke Lighthouse. It was a part of everyday life here and gave us a feeling of security that we were not even aware of until one night when it ceased to operate.

Because of this, and because of the one question asked thousands of times by visitors to the Island—"Where can I find the history of the lighthouse?"—I have put together here a brief history.

Ocracoke Lighthouse is the oldest on the Outer Banks and the shortest. It is the second oldest still in operation on the East coast of the United States. The tower is sixty-five feet high, with an overall height of seventy-five feet including the lantern. The tower is built of brick with hand-spread mortar covering the exterior walls. The walls at the base of the tower are five feet thick. The eight-thousand-candle-power fixed white electric light is visible for fourteen miles. It was built in 1823 to replace a lighthouse on Shell Castle Island which became useless because of shifting channels and sand bars.

The present lighthouse and a three-room keeper's quarters were constructed in 1823. The keeper's quarters have been expanded twice to make two living quarters which are now occupied by rangers of the Cape Hatteras National Park. The lighthouse itself is essentially unchanged except for updating of equipment. Thousands of visitors visit the site each year. It is one of the most picturesque spots on the Island.

ELLEN FULCHER CLOUD
MARCH 1993

ACKNOWLEDGMENTS

The list of people to be thanked for the publication of this booklet is endless. First on the list is Sally Newell, who was so determined that I publish this book, that she established Live Oak Publications. Thanks to Willis Slane, Agnes Wren, Paulette Chitwood, and Jennie Micket of Live Oak Publications for their support and work in getting it published. Thanks to Chief Peter Stone of the United States Coast Guard for his support during the "Window Heist" and for not having us arrested; and to Tom Hartman and Bebe Woody of the Cape Hatteras National Park for backing us all the way. Thanks to Mr. William F. Sherman of the Civil Reference Branch, National Archives, for his help in providing much needed research material for this project. Again a special thanks to Paulette Chitwood for sharing her knowledge of design and layout and the many hours she spent working on this project. Thanks to my mother who never complained when she was left to watch TV alone while I buried myself in papers. To all my friends who kept insisting that this booklet needed to be written, thanks!

EFC

Ocracoke Lighthouse
photographed by Aycock Brown in the 1950s.

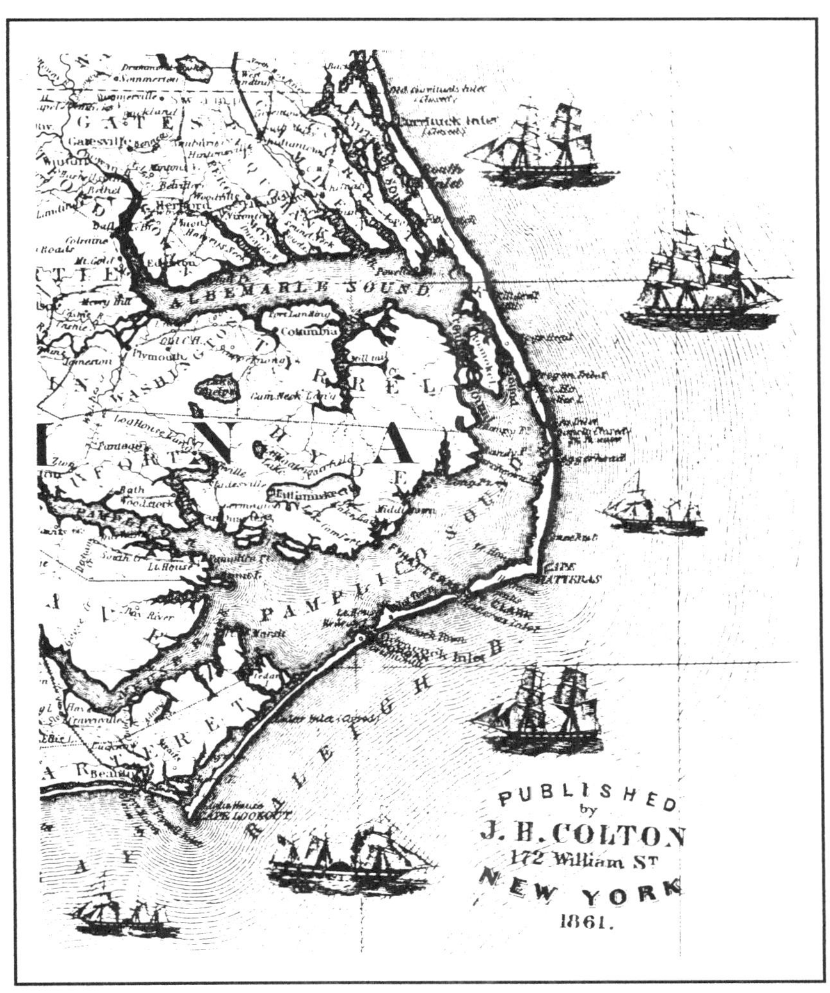

Colton 1861

Courtesy of the Library of Congress, Washington

W.P. Cumming, *North Carolina in Maps* (Raleigh: State Department of Archives and History, 1966), Plate I.

CHAPTER 1

Ocracoke Lighthouse

Ocracoke Inlet just south of Ocracoke Island was the main and most important inlet on the North Carolina coast from the early 1700s to the mid 1800s. Through this inlet came our trade and contact with the outside world. Two-thirds if not three-fourths of the commerce of North Carolina passed through Ocracoke Inlet, not less than fifteen thousand sail of vessels annually (1824).[1] It was the only inlet that remained open and at the same site while others filled in and washed out again in another location.

In 1715 an act was passed by the colonial assembly to settle and maintain pilots at Ocracoke Inlet, "it being the only port with sufficient depth of water for ships of Burden between Topsail and the Virginia capes."[2] Though the inlet remained open, the sand bars and shoals shifted, making it dangerous to enter without the aid of a pilot.

Crossing the bar at night was almost impossible, for, when there is no moon, these Outer Banks and surrounding waters are the darkest known to mankind. In 1789, because of the danger to shipping, the North Carolina General Assembly passed an act to erect a lighthouse on Ocracoke Island. On September 13, 1790, William Williams, John Williams, Joseph Williams, William Howard, Jr., and Henry Garrish deeded one acre of land to the State of North Carolina for the purpose of erecting the lighthouse.[3] The deed stated that if a lighthouse was not erected by January of 1801, the deed would be void.

However, in November of the same year, the federal government assumed the responsibility of construction and maintenance of lighthouses from the states. The construction of a light on Ocracoke Island was delayed,[4] and on March 28, 1792, it was ordered that the secretary of the treasury, "inquire into, and report to congress at their next session, the expediency of erecting a light-house on Ocracoke Island, or elsewhere, near the entrance of Ocracoke Inlet, and an estimate of the probable expense."[5] Upon learning of the proposed construction of the light on Ocracoke Island, fifty-seven pilots, masters of vessels, owners of vessels, and merchants trading in and out of the inlet got up a petition requesting it be built on Shell Castle Rock rather than on Ocracoke Island.

John Gray Blount and John Wallace operated a shipping

company on Shell Castle, as well as a store, tavern, a lightering business, and two large warehouses. On May 13, 1794, Congress approved construction of the lighthouse on Shell Castle which was located just inside Ocracoke Inlet. On May 23, 1795, an invitation for bids was published in the *North Carolina Gazette*. The tower was to be constructed of wood and covered with shingles, pyramid-shaped, 54$^1/_2$ feet high, and set on a ten-foot-deep submerged stone foundation. There was to be a six-foot lantern and a three-foot dome. H. Dearborn was awarded the contract, and the lighthouse was completed in 1798 on a small piece of land deeded to the federal government by John Wallace and John Gray Blount in 1797.[6] A transcription of the deed found in an old unnumbered deed book, Carteret County, North Carolina, Register of Deeds, follows.

> Carteret County 29 November 1797
>
> John Gray Blount of Washington, NC and John Wallace of Shell Castle, NC to the United States of America for $200 Land for the purpose expressed in an Act of Assembly of the year 1794 entitled an Act for ceding to the United States the Jurisdiction of certain land on Shell Castle Island: in the Harbor of Ocracoke a certain lot on Shell Castle at the Easternmost end thereof and to run along the rock to the Westward with Wallace Channel, seventy feet, then to beginning. With the stipulation that the U.S. shall not permit goods to be stored, a tavern to be kept, to be no retailed or merchandise to be carried on, on sd lot, or suffer any person to reside on or make that a stand from which they may either pilot or lighter vessels.
>
> J.G. Blount
> John Wallace

This 1798 light was soon rendered useless, as the shifting of sand bars and channels made it a distance of one mile from the main channel. Still the light remained in operation until it was destroyed by lightning on August 16, 1818. On May 15, 1820, fourteen thousand dollars was appropriated for a light vessel to be stationed in Ocracoke Inlet to replace the Shell Castle light. The light vessel proved unsatisfactory also and on May 7, 1822, twenty thousand dollars was approved for construction of a lighthouse on Ocracoke Island.[7]

The present lighthouse was constructed in 1823 by Noah Porter of Massachusetts at a cost of $11,359.35, which included the cost of the keeper's quarters, a one-story three-room brick house. The land on which the light was constructed was purchased from Jacob Gaskill for fifty dollars.[8]

The following is a description of navigational lights, etc, used by ships on entering Ocracoke Inlet.

> [Blount]—W.S.W. from Cape Hatteras, 8 leagues distant, is Ocracoke Inlet, on the bar of which are 9 feet of water; this bar is subject to change, and should not be entered without a pilot.
>
> At the entrance, on Ocracoke Island, a lighthouse is erected, exhibiting a revolving light, which you leave on your starboard hand entering the inlet. The time of each revolution is two minutes. It is elevated 75 feet above the water.
>
> A floating light is stationed within the point of the 9 feet shoal, near Teache's Hole Swash. She is moored in 2 fathoms water, with the light on Ocracoke bearing S.E. distance 2 3/4 miles, Shell Castle bearing S.W. 1/2 W., 4 1/2 miles, and the light-boat at the S.W. Straddle W. by S. 9 miles. A bell will be toiled [tolled] at intervals in thick and foggy weather.[9]

CHAPTER 2

Lighthouse Maintenance

The Treasury Department was the federal branch that was assigned responsibility for managing and maintaining lighthouses. The particulars that follow are from material found in the National Archives in Washington, D.C.[10] The style of the original documents has been preserved.

1854—At Ocracoke Island a fourth-order Fresnel fixed white light was substituted for the old reflecting illuminating apparatus.

1855—Ocracoke. The keepers dwelling and tower at this station were thoroughly repaired in March 1855. The Ocracoke Channel light-vessel and Beacon Island light-house were intended as a range to cross the Ocracoke bar at night in safety.

In consequence of the formation of shoals inside the bar, that range never has been, nor can it be now obtained. Should it be attempted to cross the bar by bringing these lights in a direct line, a vessel would certainly strike on the reef, with every chance of inevitable destruction.

It is possible that a range might be obtained by having two light-vessels in place of the house and one light-vessel, but the channel in which one of them would have to be moored is so subject to change that its continuance would, I fear, be of short duration. I would recommend that the two lights in question be discontinued, after sufficient notice to be given, and that the Ocracoke Channel light-vessel be stationed off the Northwest end of Royal Shoal, where a light is so much needed, until the screw-pile light-house, for which an appropriation has been made, is erected.

1856—New illuminating apparatus has been placed in the following light-houses, in this district, during the past year, viz. Hog Island, New Point, Comfort, Pools Island, Turkey Point, Sharps Island, Pamlico Point, Fishing Battery, Clay Island, Blackstone Island, the two at North Point, and Beacon Island.

1857—The Ocracoke Channel light-vessel, and the Beacon Island light-house, at the same place, have several times, been reported by this board as useless, and their discontinuance has been recommended. This recommendation is again respectfully renewed. DISCONTINUED "under the operation of the 3rd section of the act of Congress approved March 3, 1859."

1858—Beacon Island, inside of Ocracoke Inlet, brick tower, 38 feet elevation, built in 1853. Fixed, 6th-order lens light, refitted in 1855. Light on Keepers dwelling; designed as a range with light-vessel for the channel.

1860—New lanterns have been placed at Back River, Point Lookout, and Ocracoke light-houses. The substitution of Franklin for Valve lamps is going on.

1862—Ocracoke, tower standing, lens, &c., removed. [Editor's note: The Confederates removed the light from tower during the Civil War to prevent the Union ships from using it for navigation.]

1863—The light-house at Roanoke Marshes, Northwest Point of Royal Shoal, Croatan, Cape Lookout, and Ocracoke have been refitted and the lights re-exhibited.

1868—Ocracoke—A large portion of the tower has been recemented, and whitewashed two coats. Lantern and all wood in keepers dwelling and tower painted inside and out, two coats; lantern deck and sashes and frames repaired; stairways renovated extensively, putting in 33 feet of newel 14 inches diameter; one side of roof of keepers dwelling reshingled and other side repaired; fire-hearths and brick walks around the house relaid; plaster repaired in every room; also door, sashes, and hardware; floors repaired where necessary, and whitewashed.

1869—Ocracoke—The slight repairs required at this station have been made and it is now in fine order.

1883—Ocracoke, North side of Ocracoke Inlet, North Carolina. The old fence was removed and 1,200 feet of new paling fence substituted. The plaster in the dwelling was renewed, two new floors were laid, the lot was graded, and various minor repairs were made. The station is now in excellent order.

1899—Ocracoke, entrance to Ocracoke Inlet, N.C.
New model fourth-order lamps were supplied. Various repairs were made.

1903—Ocracoke, seacost of North Carolina.
In November 1902 a plank walk was laid from the dwelling to the tower.

1904—Ocracoke, seacoast of North Carolina.
A small wood shed was built in January. Some 324 running feet of fencing was erected. Various repairs were made.

On April 2, 1930, the lighthouse property on Ocracoke Island consisted of;

1 Lighthouse	$16,050
1 Oilhouse	500
1 Dwelling	5,670
1 Dwelling	7,000
1 Coal Shed	400
Total	$29,620

The appraised value of the land was $1000.[11]

CHAPTER 3

Ocracoke Lightkeepers

The following is a list of some of the keepers appointed at Ocracoke between 1847 and the last keeper who retired in 1929, as well as information about them gleaned primarily from the United States Population Census. I say "some of the keepers" because the records I've found do not cover the period prior to 1847, and therefore do not cover all of them.

Names of Some of the Keepers Appointed at Ocracoke

STATION	KEEPERS	ANL. SALARY	WHEN APPOINTED
Ocracoke	John Harker	$400	Oct. 2, 1847
"	Thomas Styron	400	Sept. 1853
"	Wm. J. Gaskill	400	Aug. 1860
"	Ellis Howard	560	1862-1897-died
"	J. Wilson Gillikin	560	1897-1898
"	Tillman F. Smith	552	1898
"	A.B. Hooper		1910
"	Wesley Austin		1912-1929
"	J.M. Burrus		Oct. 1929

John Harker
Keeper of Ocracoke Lighthouse
1847–1853

John Harker was appointed keeper of Ocracoke Lighthouse on 2 Oct. 1847 with a salary of $400 per year.[12] He is listed in the U.S. Federal Census of Ocracoke in 1850 as lightkeeper.

John is listed as being 26 years of age. In the house with him were Elizabeth Harker 27, William Harker 29, and Harriet Harker 26. By 1860 the family was living in Straits District, Carteret County, North Carolina. The household members were the same as in 1850, which might mean they were all brothers and sisters, since there were no children listed as being born in the ten-year period. I found no marriage records for these people.

Thomas Styron
Keeper of Ocracoke Lighthouse
1853–1860

Thomas Styron was appointed keeper of Ocracoke Lighthouse in September of 1853 to replace John Harker. He was keeper for seven years.[13] It is not certain which Thomas this was. In the 1850 census there was a Thomas Styron, age 53, and his son Thomas, age 29. Thomas Sr.'s occupation is listed as a boatman, and there is no occupation listed for Thomas Jr. Both are married and have a family. Both Thomas Styrons are listed in 1860, which was the year William Gaskill was appointed keeper. Neither Styron nor Gaskill was listed as a lightkeeper.

William J. Gaskill
Keeper of Ocracoke Lighthouse
1860–1862

William Gaskill was appointed keeper of Ocracoke Lighthouse in August of 1860 to replace Thomas Styron.[14] He was keeper for only two years before being replaced by Ellis Howard. He was listed in the 1860 census as being 48 years of age, married, wife Ann, age 45. Also listed were five children. Matilda 17, William 15, Robert 12, Zelpha 9, and Sam P. 6.

Enoch Ellis Howard
Keeper of Ocracoke Lighthouse
1862–1897

Ellis was appointed keeper of Ocracoke Light in 1862 with an annual salary of $560, which was still his annual income when he died in 1897,[15] thirty-five years later. Ellis Howard was born on Ocracoke on October 28, 1833, the son of Solomon Howard and Lovey Tolson. He married Cordelia Williams, also of Ocracoke. They had two children. Ellis remained keeper of the light until his death. He, his wife, and daughter are seen in photographs of the keeper's quarters on pages 12 and 13.

J. Wilson Gillikin
Keeper of Ocracoke Lighthouse
1897–1898

I have found no information on Keeper Gillikin. He was keeper for less than a year and was not living at Ocracoke when the 1900 census was taken.

The photos on the following pages were made as part of the May 24, 1893, survey of the Ocracoke Lighthouse reservation during the time of Keeper Ellis Howard.

(Page 12) Taken from "camera station no. 1" as noted on the plat. The surveyor and his camera can be seen at "camera station no. 2" near the base of the lighthouse itself, the keeper's quarters and the trees. Whitewash was a mixture of lime, whiting, size, water, etc. Traditionally on Ocracoke, molasses was added as well. As paint is used today, whitewash was used in past times to create a neat appearance on buildings. Whitewash also kept bugs from the trees. For a better appearance, whitewash on Ocracoke was applied to trees only to a height that matched that of the fence.

Keeper Ellis Howard and family standing by the keeper's quarters. This photo was made from "camera station no. 2."

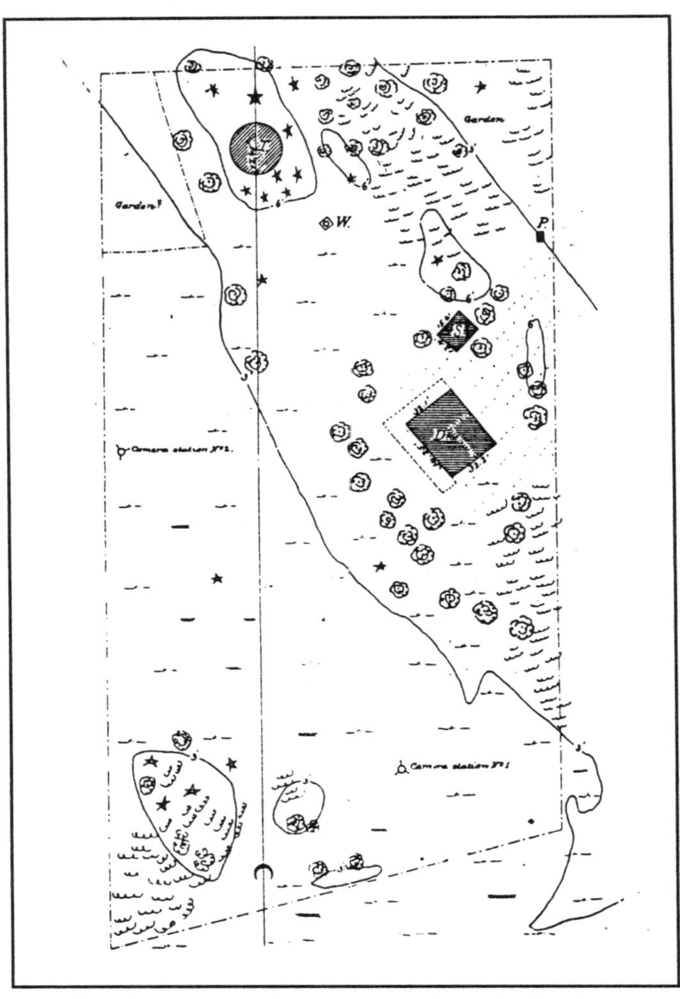

EXPLANATIONS: Datum = Assumed mean low water; T = Tower, brick; D = Dwelling, brick, roof shingle. Ht. floor 7.2'; S = Store house or shop, frame, shingle roof, wood foundation; W = Well, walled, inside diameter 2.9'; P = Privy, frame, wood foundation.

(Plat) The actual 1893 physical survey showing the area enclosed by fence, site of the light, and location of buildings, high land, marsh, gardens, and trees.

Keeper Gillikin made the first entry in the Lightkeepers Logbook found in the National Archives of History, Washington, D.C.[16] All entries were weather related except the following six.

June 6, 1897 — Schooner *Cora* arrived from West Indies.

April 6, 1898 — The schooner *S. Warren Hall* was wrecked just inside of the bar in Ocracoke Inlet about 2 Oclock yesterday loaded with shingles, from Georgetown, S.C. The crew was rescued by the crew of Portsmouth Life-Saving Station.

July 3, 1898 — Keeper left to go to Baltimore to see doctor.

July 10, 1898 — Keeper returned to station 7 am.

July 24, 1898 — Keeper left station at 4 pm to go to Washington.

July 29, 1898 — Keeper returned 6 am.

Tilmon F. Smith
Keeper of Ocracoke Lighthouse
1898–1910

Tilmon F. Smith was appointed keeper of Ocracoke Lighthouse in 1898. He is listed in the 1900 census as being 48 years of age. His wife was Sabra S., age 47. They had two boarders living in their home; Nora D. Smith, age 21, and Emagene Austin, age 13. Tilmon and Sarah had been married twenty-four years.

Entries by Keeper Smith other than weather and work done on station:[17]

Oct. 8, 1898 — The tender *Violet* arrived at the station 3 pm. The mate of the tender delivered to the keeper 3 cord of wood and 2 tons of coal.

Oct. 15, 1898 — The keeper whitewashes his cow stable and chicken house today.

Feb. 4, 1899 — The lighthouse engineer visited the station today and took away the old lamps and left 3 new ones.

Feb. 12, 1899 — Snow storm. Keeper visited the light several times, from sunset to sunrise to keep the interior of the lantern glass clear of ice.

Jun. 8, 1899 — Keeper sick, Mr. John Spencer substituted.

1900

Mar. 17-30 — Keeper sick.

Jul. 25 — Keeper received a telegram that his mother was dead

2pm — Left station 2:30 pm for Hatteras.

1901

Jun. — Tender *Holly* arrived in the harbor to work buoys.

Jul. 20 — Keeper left to go to Washington to visit sick wife.

Jul. 26 — Keeper is sick. Mr. George T. Willis substituted.

Jul. 28 — Keeper is sick.

Oct. 26 — Keeper left station to go to Rocky Mt. N.C.

1902

Jan. 1st. to Feb. 9th. — Keeper reported that he could not see reflection of search light from Diamond Shoal light.

May 1 — Keeper left station today for medical treatment.

May 30 — Keeper returned to station today.

Nov. 18 — commenced building walk from dwelling to tower.

1903

May 4 — Keeper and wife left at 11 am in answer to a telegram summoning them to their daughter in Washington, N.C.

May 12 — Keeper returned to station 4 pm.

1905

Feb. 25 — Keeper left 8:30 am to go to Bluff Shoal Light returned 4 pm.

A. B. Hooper
Keeper of Ocracoke Lighthouse
1910–1912

Hooper was appointed keeper of Ocracoke Lighthouse in 1910. He is listed as living at Ocracoke in 1910; his occupation is listed as lighthouse keeper. His wife was Mariah and they had been married for 25 years. Living with him were the following children: Richard, 23, son; Frederic, 20, son; Robert 15, son; and Hattie, 11, cousin.

Records in Logbook referring to Hooper were two approvals for leave of absence, one on August 2, 1910, the other July 31, 1911.

Captain Leon Wesley Austin
Keeper of Ocracoke Lighthouse
1912–1929

Capt. Austin was born at Hatteras, North Carolina, in 1864, the son of Isaac Farrow Austin and Sarah Ann Midgette. He married Isabelle Barnett, also of Hatteras. Wesley spent his late boyhood and early manhood on windjammers plying the east coast.

Capt. Leon Wesley Austin was transferred to Ocracoke Station from Corolla Station November 28, 1912, when he was forty-eight years old. He retired from service September 30, 1929, after over forty-five years with the Lightkeeper's Service.

He entered the U.S. Lighthouse Service in 1885, serving on tenders as a freshman, then transferred to Cape Hatteras Lighthouse as third assistant keeper, where he served for eight years, earning a salary of $450 per year. In 1893 he was appointed first assistant keeper at Corolla, earning $500 a year. In 1913 he was promoted to keeper and transferred to Ocracoke Lighthouse where he retired in 1929 with over forty-five years service. Wesley and Isabelle had four children and made Ocracoke their home when he retired.

See Chapter Four for abstracts from Keeper Austin's logbook.

Capt. Joe Burrus
Last Keeper of Ocracoke Lighthouse
1929–1946

Capt. Burrus was the keeper of Ocracoke Lighthouse for sixteen years. He retired from the Lighthouse Service with forty-five years' service as keeper of lighthouses in Virginia

This photograph of "Captain Joe," as he was called, was made at the time of his retirement in 1946 and appeared in the Raleigh, North Carolina, *News and Observer*. He is looking out over Silver Lake from the top of the lighthouse.

Captain Joseph Merrit Burrus in full dress uniform. Captain Burrus was the last keeper of Ocracoke Lighthouse, serving from 1929 to 1946. Note the lighthouse insignia on the cap.

and North Carolina. His first paycheck back in 1903 was thirty dollars per month.

Over the years he was stationed at Tangier, Virginia, Thimble Shoal, Virginia, and Diamond Shoal Lightship, Cape Lookout, Croatan, Oliver's Reef, Bluff Shoal, and Ocracoke, all in North Carolina. His service at Ocracoke was from 1929 to 1946. He was the last keeper of Ocracoke Lighthouse. There was no longer a need for a keeper after automation of the lights.

Joe was born at Hatteras, North Carolina, as was his wife Eleanor Oden. They were the parents of six children and made Ocracoke their home after retirement.

Keeper Joe Burrus made but few entries in the logbook. It has been said that he refused to make entries because it was a waste of good time. He had more important things to do.

This photograph is an aerial view looking from the Ocracoke Lighthouse toward Silver Lake. It was taken by Aycock Brown in the 1950s. The docks of the World War II Navy base can be seen at the top of the photo.

CHAPTER 4

Keeper Wesley Austin's Logbook 1912–1929

The information recorded here was copied from microfilm from the National Archives in Washington, D.C. It covers the time period in which Wesley Austin was the Keeper of Ocracoke Lighthouse, 1912–1929. The logbook has an entry every day, which for the most part tells the weather for that day or that Captain Austin whitewashed the fence, tower, house, or outbuildings. I have tried here to report all other information as it was recorded in the logbook. I have copied it word for word as it was written, including misspelled words.

EFC

1912

Nov. 28th Reported for duty as Keeper of Ocracoke Light Station, Nov. 25, 1912—Wesley Austin, Keeper.

Dec. 13th At 2:30 am Vapor failed to burn, needling would not do eny good. Substituted oil lamp untill sun rise.

1913

Jan. 3rd Had to take the vapor lamp out substitute oil lamp.

Feb. 4th Vaporizer leaked so bad had to substitute oil lamp.

Feb. 15th " " " " " " " " "

Feb. 16th " " " " " " " " "

Feb. 20th Chief construction enginer, H. B. Bowerman arrived at station at 3:30 pm on the 20th left at 8 am the 21st. for Cape Hatteras Light Station.

One of the tenders used to transport supplies to lighthouses on the North Carolina coast. This is the tender that transported Captain Wesley Austin from Corolla Station to Ocracoke in 1912.

Mar. 4th Painted roof of dwelling.

Mar. 6th Light burned good til 1 am—1am to sunrise falt.

Mar. 16th Painted window shutters on dwelling.

Mar. 29th Vapor light leaked bad substituted oil lamp at 7:45

May 28th Repair party arrived to station 2 pm and put cement coating on top of tower, repaired fence planks, walks and out buildings, left station.

July 10th The four masted schooner *V. Josephine* of Baltimore Md. went ashore at Ocracoke Inlet on the morning of July 10th 1913 at 4 am. Assistance was rendered by Ocracoke and Portsmouth Lifesaving Stations. Cause of Casualty—Ocracoke Light was mistaken for Bodie Island Light.

July 22nd From 3 to 3:45 am Light was very dim nozzle pretty stoped up.

Sept. 3rd Hurrican on the night of the 2nd and morning of 3rd. From NE to SE blew and washed down part of the fence, plank walks, slightly damaged by sea tide and did very much damage to trees inside reservation.

Sept. 4th. Cleaning litter out of reservation—also on the 6, 7, 8, 9, & 10th.

Sept. 11th Repaired water closet.

Sept. 13th Repaired plank walk

Sept. 15th Repaired fences

Sept. 17th Touched up dwelling with whitewash

Oct. 2nd Inspected this date, found in good condition.

Oct. 16th Tender *Holly* delivered anual supplies to station. Keeper delivered to tender *Holly* 120 oil cans and 2–class can buoy.

Oct. 24th Referring to report of service rendered by you during the storm of Sept. 2 & 3, 1913, for preserving the government property under your charge and in giving shelter to the residents of Ocracoke Island, who were driven from their homes by the high tides, you are commended for the service rendered on the occasion in question, which fact will be noted on the records as part of your official history.

—*Through, Commissioner of Lighthouses.*

Oct. 25th Commenced to whitewash outside of tower. worked 2hr

26th " " " " " "
worked 8 hrs.

27th " " " " " "
3 hrs

Nov. 1st Finished scraping and whitewashing out side of tower

3rd Painted outside of lantern of tower

4th Painted lantern deck of tower

6th Whitewashed fence

Dec. 2nd Sub oil lamp, vaporizer leaked at joint, also 2, 3, 4, 5, 6th.

11th Tender *Holly* supplyed 3 tons coal, 2 cords wood.

12th Light burned good all night—new preheater.

1914

Jan. 3rd One redhead killed against tower.

Feb. 23rd Repair crew arrived at station at 8 am to build new oil house.

Mar. 10th Painted outside kitchen wall

16th Painted boxing around eves of dwelling.

17th Painted outside of dwelling.
26th Cleaning old paint off of inside of lantern.

Apr. 6th Whitewashed inside of tower.
17th Painted stairway inside of tower

Jun. 5th Filled in yard with mud from ditch to hold the grass in back yard.
26th Tender *Holly* delivered annual supplies.

Jul. 7th Keeper left station 6 am on leave of absence
15th Keeper returned to station 10 am from leave 8 days 4 hours.
31st Station inspected, found in excellent condition.

Aug. 1914

EFFICENCY STARS—AUG. 18, 1914
KEEPER OCRACOKE LIGHT STATION

You are informed that you have been awarded an efficency star, you are therefore entitled to wear the efficency star for the succeding fiscal year beginning July 1st, 1914. Shall be worn in a manor describeed in the uniform manuel.

Tender *Holly* delivered two cords of wood and three tons of coal to station at 3 pm.

1915

Mar. 22nd Repair party arrived at station 8 am, minor repairs and left station at 4 pm.

June 1st Copy; Lighthouse Inspector, Baltimore, Md.

Sir; I write to tell you there are some complaints with the captains of the vessels now trading from Ocracoke in regards to the beacon light no. 1155, Swash Channel, not showing effecient light at night and that a white light would give better satisfaction.

Wesley Austin, Keeper

June 7th Inspected station—condition very good, *King*

July 3rd Keeper left station at 2 pm returned at 5 pm
12th William Venson arrived to station at 1 pm installed recording thermometer in tower and left station at 10:30 am

Aug. 13, 1915.

Sept. 3rd Needled lamp at 8 pm.
18th Tender *Laurel* delivered supplies to station.
20th Painted outside lantern of tower and lantern deck.

Oct. 11th Painted inside of lantern of tower and lantern floor

Dec. 17th At 5:45 am vapor lamp worked bad, was necessary to substitute oil lamp until daylight.
24th Keeper left station at 5:45 pm to attend church, returned to station at 7:05 pm.

1916

Mar. 4th Alarm bell called at 3:35 am, light was all right. Needled lamp and adjusted the alarm.

Apr. 3rd Repair party arrived to station at 8 am. tuck out part off plank walks and kitchen.
4th Put in forms for concreet walks
5th Repaired kitchen and made forms for top of cistern
6th Repaired kitchen and concreet top of cisterrn
7th Built new privey and concreet foundation
8th Building concreet walks
10th Taking up plank walks for cencreet
11th Building concreet walks and closet in tower
12th Building concreet walks
13th Repair party finished work, left station 9:30 am
14th Cleaning reservation

15th Cleaning up reservation
16th Sunday
17th Whitewashing inside walls of tower
19th Painting outbuildings of station
21st Taking out forms around walks
22nd Cleaning reservation
23rd Sunday
24th Painting outbuildings
25th Painting closet in tower
26th Painting porch to kitchen
27th Whitewashing outside of tower
29th Cleaning elluminating apparatus
30th Sunday
May 23rd Fixing chicking lot
(all other days spent cleaning painting & whitewashing, house, fence and tower).
31st Painted hot house

Jun 1st Pollashed elluminating apparatus
10th Pollashed brass articles, lamps etc.
15th No lights visible except-Swash and Cockle shoal Beacons
16th Wind and rain badly beat off whitewash on outside wall of tower.
18th Keeper left station at 10:30 am to attend church, returned 12 noon.
21st SW Point, Bluffshoal and Beacon vissible
25th Keeper left station at 2:30 pm returned 3 pm
28th Tender *Laural* delivered annual supplies
29th Stacking up annual supplies and taking inventory
30th Made out annual property return

Jul 4th Wind and rain badly beat off thermomoner pen caught—behind bad from 7 pm to 10 pm

5th Keeper sick all day no work done
6th Cleaned up in tower
7th Keeper left station at 6:35 am on leef July 7, 1916
8th Worked on the tower burnt oil lamp
9th Act keeper left station at 10:45 to attend church returned 2:15.
11th Tuck out oil lamp
12th Went to the post office for the mail
14th Hot and sultry all day—no work done
16th Left station 10:30 to attend church returned 4:15
17th Left station 3:30 for the mail returned 5:30
19th Rain and win storm from NE vapor bad from 6:30-7:30
24th House open for ventilation
26th Keeper returned to station July 26, 1916 at 1:30 pm

Aug 1st Cutting weeds around fence
2nd Cutting grass inside reservation
4th Scowerd staresteps in tower
6th Keeper left station at 10:30 to attend church, returned 12 noon.
Aug 7th Scowerd porch floors of dwelling
9th United States Coast and Geodetic survay put in bench mark at tower door.

1917

Jan 15th Owing to bad weather no work don at station at 7:20 pm lamp worked so bad tuck out vaporizer and connection relief valve to lamp. light extinguished 30 minutes.

Feb 2nd Snowing, fresh breeze NW pm snowing fresh gale NW

3rd Owing to bad weather no work done today. lantern of tower sweted and frozed untill all inside of lantrn was iced over.

4th Keeper sick with rheumatism all day

5th Inside of lantern iced over tonight

Apr. 12th Painted black outside lantern of tower

13th Asst. supt inspected station at 4 pm

16th Put in telegraph poles inside reservation

Sep. 2nd Alarm bell called and going in tower found the lamp enveloped in red flame, turned oil off and needled lamp then the lamp burned fare untill sunrise.

Oct 3rd Installed telephone in office today

Dec 26th Rain and snow fresh breeze NE

29th Snow and rain to severe snow storm fresh gale NW

30th Snowing

31st Coast Gard telephone inspector visited station at 3:36 pm

1918

Jan lst Clear light breeze NW freezing weather

2nd Snowing, light breeze NE freezing

20th Snow

Apr 1st By order—clock turned ahead one hour 2 am March 31st.

1919

Feb 3rd Coast Guard Supt. visited station at 4:45 pm

1920

May 4th Keeper worked on his motor boat

22nd Making pickets to replace fence

25th Put in nine fence post today
26th Put in 6 fence post and one rail today
27th Put in 7 fence post
28th Made 79 pickets for fence

Jun 1st Put up guttering on dwelling
8th 75 pickets today
9th 60 pickets today
10th Made 2 gates for fence

Jul 14th Tender *Laurel* delivered supplies today

Aug 11th Light out of commission, substituted old oil lamp

Norfolk Va. June 12, 1919, 8 pm to all Coast Guard Stations from No. 101 to 191 . . . Coast Guard Stations, Lighthouse Keepers, and all petroles along the coast from Cape Henry to Cape Fear, *Keep bright lookout for submarines* for all scho rig, schooners, steam or sail painted gray, and any news from conserning subject. Keep the department informed. *This subject very important.*

signed,
Capt. Commandont
5th Navel District

Inspecter declared station in Excellent Condition;

1914 Jan 18, Jun 7, Oct 18, Apr 10, Sept 25,
1917 Apr. 13, Sept. 3,
1918 March 8th
1919 May 17th

July 7, 1916 Keeper lift station at 6:35 am on leave of absense, returned to station July 25 at 1:30 pm—period of absence 15 days, 6 hours and 55 min.

June 6th Keeper left station 8:30 am returned June 20 at 12:30 pm period of absence 12 days. and 4 hours for medical treatment.

TELEGRAM
Baltimore Md.
Aug. 5, 1920
To Wesley Austin
Ocracoke, NC

20 days leave with substance, government expence approved.
Dillon
received 9:30 pm

RECORD OF ABSENCE

1919 WESLEY AUSTIN left station 25 times; once to attend public speaking, once to carry daughter to Hatteras, once on annual leave, and 22 times to attend church.

TELEGRAMS
Department of Commerce

Send to Port Captain
Ocracoke, NC July 24, 1924
Buoy Dept.
Portsmouth, Va

All buoys relieved around Ocracoke, will load oil dryms and leave Friday enroute Washington, Kindly

Ocracoke, Oct. 18, 1927

All buoys releived around Ocracoke, complete work assigned necessary proceed Washington for coal—leave Ocracoke Wednesday-winds and sea permitting Kindly

Coast Survey Washingtonn DC
Ocracoke, Aug 21, 1927

Arrived Ocracoke twentieth. Moore

Port Captain
Ocracoke, NC July 1925
Lighthouse Dept. Portsmouth Va.

Juniper arrived Ocracoke Wednesday night condition unsuitable for buoy work—report juniper, Baltimore office

Portsmouth Bouy Dept.
Keeper Light Station
Portsmouth Va to Ocracoke Light Station, Ocracoke NC

Lighthouse tender *Speedwell* will arrive Ocraacoke Bar weather permitting, Tuesday morning Nov. 20—Make arrangement local pilot to meet pilot acknolage. Almy

Baltimore Md.
July 8, 1921

Keeper Ocracoke Light Stationn, Ocracoke, NC reply to letter of June 17, Relative Schooner—*Carroll A. Dearing.*

King

To Supt of Lighthouses
Ocracoke Light Station
Baltimore, MD
July 9, 1921

Reply to letter June 17th 1921—relative *Carroll A Derring* forwarded by mail. Keeper

Aug. 23, 1925 — Four masted schoonor *Victora S.* stranded on Ocracoke Roads about 1 am—in part from Georgetown SC to New York loaded—Pine lumber. Keeper Feb 11, 1921 Called by keeper C. G. Stationn on telephone—notifed light was out—hurridely going in tower reheated lamp 10 min—relit the light at 3:05 am—light extinguished from 2:15 to

3:05 am time extinguished about 50 min—caused by nozzle stoping up alarm bell failed to call at proper time.

Aug 11th, 1921 — Keeper left station at 7 am to meet daughter at Hatteras

Aug 12th, 1921 — Showing visitors in tower

Aug 12th, 1921 — Schooner *Message of Peace* marroned in Ocracoke Inlet just below Teaches Hole. Bouy Haling Port Nassau, NJ

Nov. 11th 1921 — American Flag Flown On Ocracoke Light Station in honor of Americans dead, from Sunrise to Sunset

July 27th 1923 — Keeper stuck a 20 penny nail in bottom of foot, making a painful wound about 1 pm. 28, 29, 30, 31, not able to work because of foot

Aug 10th 1923 — Keeper left on leave today

WESLY AUSTIN, Keeper of Ocracoke Light Station was retired from active duty in the Light House Service with the close of business Sept. 30th 1929 after 45 years, 3 months service.

Oct 11th 1929 — J. M. BURRUS reported for duty at this Station today.

Oct 29th 1929 — Light changed to electric.

CHAPTER 5

Other Lights and Lightkeepers

Other lighthouses, light vessels, and beacon lights in the vicinity of Ocracoke in Pamlico Sound were:

Light Vessels	**Lighthouses**
Pamlico Point	North West Point of Royal Shoal
Ocracoke Channel	Long Shoal
Long Shoal	Beacon Island
Pamlico Point	Brant Island
Brant Island	Harbor Island
Nine Feet Shoal	

Lighthouses and light vessels were in isolated locations, making it hard to get needed supplies. Bids were taken from those wanting to acquire the job of transporting supplies to the light vessels and stations.

The following is an ad placed in the *Republican* (newspaper published in Washington, N.C.) by the superintendent of lighthouses:

Superintendent's Office
District of Ocracoke
March 1st. 1839

Proposals will be received at this office until the 31st. day of the present month for transportation of provisions, water, wood, oil, materials, and c.—for one year, from the lst. April next, for 6 LIGHT-BOATS, stationed in Pamtico[20] Sound, N.C. viz:

LIGHT BOAT	at the mouth of Neuse River
" "	Brant Island Shoal
LIGHT BOAT	Harbour Island Bar
" "	S.W. Point of Royal Shoal
" "	Nine Feet Shoal
" "	Long Shoal

The articles required to be furnished will be delivered to Ocracoke or Portsmouth, at some store-house or landing, except the wood, which will be delivered to some landing on Neuse Bay or Pamtico[21] Sound—the transportation to be made quarterly, or oftener if required, by the superintendent, payment to be made over after the expiration of each quarter.

S. Brown
Superintendent

Before the light vessels were constructed and placed into operation, the channels were marked and advertised in a local paper. One example of these notices is listed here:

Washington Gazette
Friday, July 24, 1807

Notice:
Of buoys placed in Pamlico Sound—by DAVID WALLACE JR. who was appointed to place buoys and give their bearings . . . (bearings given) . . . PORTSMOUTH, MAY 25, 1807

Names of Some of the Keepers Appointed at Pamlico Sound Stations and Vessels[22]

Station	Keepers	Annual Salary	When Appointed
BEACON ISLAND			
	J.T. Hunter	$350	Aug. 1855
	J. Orrow	350	Feb. 1850
PAMLICO POINT			
	Lemuel Fulford	400	May 1849
	William Brinn	400	Mar. 1859
	Burton Shipp	400	
	N.W. Ireland	400	Sept. 1856
	Robert Wallace	400	Jan. 1867
	Stephen Fowler	500	July 1867
ROYAL SHOAL VESSEL			
	Anson Gaskill	500	May 1849
	Isaac W. Davis	500	Aug. 1850
	Anson Chadwick	500	May 1853
	George W. Styron	500	1854-1860
	Wallace Styron	500	Jan. 1860
NW POINT ROYAL SHOAL			
Keeper	Benj. Robinson	500	May 1857
1st asst.	L.J. Hunter	300	Jul. 1857
2nd asst.	Thomas Newby	300	Jul. 1857
2nd asst.	Judith Robinson	300	May 1859
1st asst.	Matilda Robinson	300	May 1859
Keeper	Benj. Lawrence	500	
Assistant	John W. Hill	300	
"	George Rose	300	
"	James Newbern	300	Feb. 1865
"	Thomas C. Jones	300	May 1865
"	J.J. McGourn	300	Dec. 1865
"	C.F. Austin	300	Apr. 1866

Station	Keepers	Annual Salary	When Appointed
NW POINT ROYAL SHOAL			
Assistant	Edward B. Burrus	$300	Sept. 1866
Keeper	Thomas C. Jones	600	Sept. 1866
Assistant	George Smith	300	1866
Assistant	George Mayo	300	Oct. 1866
"	Gedion Tolson	300	1867–1868
"	Mary J. Jones	300	Jan. 1867
Keeper	Oscar F. Roe	600	1878
"	Elija Dixon	440	1878
"	Charles B. Keeler	440	1878
"	James E. Harman	440	1878
Keeper	Benj. Lawrence	600	1879
Assistant	T.S. Gaskill	440	1879
"	E.S. Gaskill	440	1867–1875
Keeper	L.C. Angill	600	1885–1886
Assistant	Thos B. Spencer	440	1886–1888
Keeper	E.L. Keeler	600	Jul. 1886
Assistant	Wallace Morris	440	Jun. 1886
"	F.M. Goodwin	440	1888–1889
"	Joseph W. O'Neal	440	Mar. 1889
"	John W. O'Neal	440	1889–1890
"	Alonzo English	440	1890–1895
"	Susan D. Keeler	440	1895
HARBOR ISLAND			
Keeper	Gayer Chadwick	500	Jul. 1849
"	Oliver Chadwick	500	Apr. 1853
"	Gayer Chadwick	500	Feb. 1867
Assistant	Jeramiah Fidly	300	Feb. 1867
Keeper	W.B. Physive	600	Jul. 1867
Assistant	John Smith	400	Oct. 1867

Station	Keepers	Annual Salary	When Appointed
HARBOR ISLAND			
Assistant	Isaac Pender	$400	Jan. 1869
Keeper	David Stanton	600	Jan. 1870
Assistant	Thomas C. Davis	440	1874-1875
"	Thomas C. Davis	440	1875–1879
Keeper	Wm T. Steward	600	1877–1879
"	Martin F. Siar	600	1879
"	John T. Shipp	600	1879
Assistant	Selden D. Delmar	440	1879
"	George W. Wade	440	1879
BRANT ISLAND VESSEL			
Keeper	John S. Curtis	500	Oct. 1847
"	Christopher O'Neal	500	Sept. 1850
"	Amos Ireland	500	Jul. 1853
"	James Fountain	500	
BRANT ISLAND			
Keeper	James Fountain	500	Feb. 1864
Assistant	W. Davis	300	1864
"	John Walktin	300	1864
"	John W. Hill	300	1864
Keeper	John W. Walkin	600	Mar. 1866
Assistant	Levi Rock	400	Jun. 1866
"	Thomas Wilkein	400	1866
"	John Canuly ?	400	1866
"	Charles F. Price	400	1866
"	John F. Wilkins	400	1867
Keeper	Edward B. Hooper	600	1870
Assistant	Wade L Harvey	400	1870
Keeper	George L. Smith	600	1872
Assistant	James D. Wilkin	400	1872

Station	Keepers	Annual Salary	When Appointed
BRANT ISLAND			
Keeper	Elijah L Gaskill	$600	1873
Assistant	J.C. Johnston	600	1873
Keeper	Peter Johnston	600	1873
"	Charles B. Keeler	600	1877
Assistant	Edward S. Keeler	400	1877
"	Lazarus G. Hinnant	400	1886–1887
Keeper	Wm. J. Simmons	600	1887–1895
Assistant	Royal L. Ireland	400	1887–1895
"	Chalcendany Lewis	400	1891–1893
"	Lewis B. Austin	440	1894
"	Mrs. Lela Simmons	440	1895
Keeper	Lazarus Hinnant	600	1895–1897
Assistant	Alonzo J. English	440	1895–1900
Keeper	Robert M. Jennette	600	1897–1900
Keeper	Alonzo J. English	600	1900
Assistant	W.L. Gaskill	440	1900
LONG SHOAL LIGHT VESSEL			
Keeper	Christopher O'Neal	500	1849— appt.to Shoal
Keeper	Ronald Midgett	500	died Sept.1853
"	Samuel Pugh	500	Mar. 1852
"	Robert Robinson	500	Jul. 1853
"	M.L. Shanberg	500	——
"	L.A. Wilaon	500	1863
	Ohn Best	500	1864
LONG SHOAL STATION			
Keeper	John Best	500	May 1867
Assistant	Wm. Hooper	400	Aug. 1867
Keeper	Nasa W. Farrow	600	Sep. 1867

Station	Keepers	Annual Salary	When Appointed
LONG SHOAL STATION			
Assistant	Wm. O'Neal	$400	Oct. 1867
"	Sanderson Pain	400	Jan. 1869
"	David P. Gray	400	Jan. 1870
"	Wm. P. O'Neal	400	1870–1871
"	Francis P. Midgett	400	Jul. 1873
Keeper	Wm. H. Manley	600	1873–1876
Assistant	Marcus L. Lewis	420	1873–1876
Keeper	Elijah D. Dixon	600	1876–1878
Assistant	Edward S. Keeler	420	1876–1878
"	John J. Sharp	420	1878–1879
"	John R. Pigott	420	1878
Keeper	Augus. C. Thompson	600	1878
Assistant	John R. Pigott	420	1878

CHAPTER 6

The Great Window Heist

A First-Person Account

The Ocracoke Lighthouse and the structures within the compound were on the National Register of Historical Places long before the Village of Ocracoke became an Historical District. Approximately thirty-two thousand people visit this historical station annually. It is owned by the U.S. Coast Guard (USCG), which is responsible for the operation and maintenance of the lighthouse. The keeper's quarters are used by the National Park Service, which has the responsibility for the maintenance and upkeep in accordance with the terms of a written agreement with the U.S. Coast Guard. In 1987 the National Park Service (NPS) determined that the keeper's quarters needed major rehabilitation, and by 1990 had expended $278,000 to rehabilitate the interior of the structure.

During this time several inspections were made of the lighthouse and it was found in need of immediate preservation work to stabilize its deteriorating condition. As a result of a Bicentennial Lighthouse Grant of seventeen thousand dollars, the NPS initiated an "Historic Structures Report" to assess the structure's condition, document historic fabric, and develop a scope of work.

Near the lighthouse is a small generator house, which holds the generator that keeps the lighthouse in operation when there is a power outage. Because Ocracoke gets its power from Virginia, the island is often without electricity; if anything happens anywhere down the line, we who are at the end of the line lose power. The lighthouse had continued to glow with or without power for 165 years until 1988, when the tired, worn-out generator ceased to work. The U.S. Coast Guard decided not to replace it, as it would be less costly to install battery-driven navigational lights on the hand rails that encircled the lamp of the tower. This was done by drilling holes through the structure near the base, through which cables could be run that would operate the lights by batteries. Not only was it unsightly, it added seriously to the weakening of the structure.

The presence of the light from Ocracoke Lighthouse had given the residents of Ocracoke, as well as the captains of ships off shore, a feeling of security that even we were unaware of until the first power outage. None of us realized that, when an outage occurred, our first reaction was to immediately look in the direction of the lighthouse. A feeling of desertion and insecurity must have swept the island, for the power outage was the topic of the next day's conversation. The two small battery-operated lights that had been installed on the rail were on and the lighthouse was in darkness. The sight was viewed with anger and disbelief.

In February of 1989 a contract was put in operation to paint the lighthouse and repair the windows and door. The old wood-clad windows were removed and vinyl Andersen windows with snap-in muntins (which are in violation of the *Secretary of the Interior's Standards* for historic structures) were installed.

Upon learning of this, I contacted two friends, who joined me, and promptly took action, demanding that the contractor cease work. The contractor disregarded our demands, but we were able to make a quick inspection of the work being done.

Not only were the windows a violation by style and mate-

These photos show the battery-operated navigational lights which were installed on the hand rails that encircle the lamp itself. To cut costs, the U.S.C.G. installed these lights instead of replacing the worn-out generator.

This photograph shows the vinyl Andersen windows with snap-in muntins which had been installed in place of the original six-over-six wooden windows. These vinyl windows were in violation of the *Secretary of the Interior's Standards* for historic structures.

rial, but they were not large enough for the opening in the structure! The openings had been framed up with 4x4 material to make the windows adaptable. Inquiring about the old windows, we learned that they were to be sent to Portsmouth, Virginia, to be destroyed and were at this time inside the ground level of the lighthouse.

We left the premises in order to make some phone calls and inform the proper authorities. We talked to the U.S. Coast Guard, National Park Service, State Historical Preservation Society, and Congressman Walter P. Jones's office. All agreed that these acts were in violation of Section 106 of the National Historical Preservation Act of 1966.

In one of those phone calls, I was made aware of a letter dated May 27, 1987, two years prior, from the Department of Cultural Resources in Raleigh, North Carolina, to the United States Coast Guard in Portsmouth, Virginia, part of which follows:

> We seriously question the need to replace all windows and frames as specified in Section 8G. Our photographs of Ocracoke Lighthouse indicate that the existing wood windows and frames are in fair-to-good condition. The total replacement of all window frames and sash with new vinyl-clad or aluminum-clad units with snap-in muntins would be in violation of the *Secretary of the Interior's Standards* for use in either the door or windows of the Ocracoke Lighthouse.
>
> We recommend that each existing window frame and sash be carefully inspected for its condition. Any deteriorated elements of the window frames, such as sills, stops, jams, and lintels should be repaired or replaced to match the existing detailing. All sash which are in sound condition should be repaired and glazed as needed. Frames or sash which are too deteriorated to be repaired should be replaced with new frames or sash which have been milled or fabricated to match

the existing ones. Any new replacement sash should be of true six-light construction, and identical to the existing sash. Snap-in muntins are not acceptable.

Realizing that the workmen at the lighthouse at that very moment were in direct violation of all official instructions for the project and that we had confirmation of this fact, we returned to the lighthouse to inspect the windows which had been removed from the structure. Upon arrival we found the door of the lighthouse had been secured by twisting wire around the latch. With much protest from the contractor, we opened the door and found the windows to be in excellent condition. We proceeded to take the windows to our vehicle in order to hold them for safe keeping, ignoring the demands of the contractor to put them back.

Realizing, as we drove off, the seriousness of removing federal property without permission, we decided to call all authorities, both state and federal, to inform them of our act and demand they take action at once to render support and cease the destruction of this historical structure.

By late afternoon a meeting had been arranged for the following Wednesday with the National Park Service, our Hyde County Commissioner, and several U.S.C.G. Officers, including Commander Malrose and Lt. McCaffrey, both of Cleveland, Ohio, who had the contract with the civilian contractor. I had had several conversations earlier in the day with Malrose or McCaffrey. I felt they were neither cooperative nor courteous; on two occasions they refused to take my calls.

At the meeting, Commander Malrose and Lt. McCaffrey, who had flown in from Cleveland, heard our complaints and were informed of the seriousness of disregarding the regulations for compliance with Section 106 of the Advisory Coun-

This cartoon by Butsie Brown was circulated through the village of Ocracoke for months after the incident and was sold in some of the gift shops and the Art Co-op.

Ocracoke Preservation Society, Inc.

P.O. Box 491, Ocracoke, North Carolina 27960-0456

FEB 8,1989

U.S. COAST GUARD
OCRACOKE, NC 27960

OCRACOKE PRESERVATION SOCIETY HAS IN IT'S POCESSION FOR SAFE KEEPING, EIGHT SECTIONS, (FOUR WINDOWS) FROM THE OCRACOKE LIGHTHOUSE, THAT WERE REMOVED WHEN THE NEW WINDOWS WERE INSTALLED.

Ellen F. Cloud
ELLEN F. CLOUD
TRUSTEE

Received by [signature] Date 09 FEB 89
I hereby sign for this particular reciept.

The U.S. Coast Guard asked for a signed statement to the effect, that we had the windows, which relieved them from responsibility. This is a copy of the statement.

cil. This law was clearly explained by a specialist on restoration of historical structures at this meeting.

After hearing our complaints, Commander Malrose agreed to have windows milled like the old ones to replace the vinyl ones and to purchase a generator and remove the lights on the rail.

In April of the following year, after seeing no activity that would make the situation right, I called Commander Malrose, who denied making such agreements. He said he planned to do nothing until the summer of 1990. He was told that we wanted the lights removed before August 7th, which had been designated as National Lighthouse Day, and that we could live with the windows until after that date. His reply was short and to the point, saying; "I wish you luck. I have no plans for the near future to do any of this work."

I called Congressman Jones's office, and talked with Mr. Floyd Lupton, who said he would get right on it. At 5:30 pm Mr. Lupton called me back to inform me that a generator would be purchased and shipped that day. The battery-operated lights would be off before August 7th. He stated that the windows would take longer because they had to be milled.

As promised by Congressman Jones's office, the generator was replaced and the lights removed from the rail, though not in time for the August 7th celebration, for the generator house had to be restored. The old original windows have now been reworked and are back in place within the structure. The National Park Service is to be given credit for this, for it was their restoration department that restored the windows, but I must add that the United States Coast Guard paid the bill.

This act was a startling realization of the importance of getting the lighthouse placed under the control of the National Park Service. Several contacts have been made in an attempt to achieve this goal. The Coast Guard is anxious to transfer the structure to the National Park, but they must retain ownership of the light or lens at the top, since all aids to navigation are their responsibility. The National Park wants the ownership of the structure but must wait and go through all the governmental red tape necessary for such a transfer.

I in no way mean to criticize the U.S. Coast Guard, for they play a most important part in the lives of all the Bankers. They risk their lives every day in order to save others. Most of the male population of Ocracoke has served in or been part of the Coast Guard or Life Saving Service, or in some way been helped by the service. It is a branch of the military service that we hold in great admiration and pride.

The Coast Guard's responsibility is to *save lives and not historical structures*. It is for this reason we recommend the lighthouse be placed under the control of the National Park, whose main priority is the restoration of such structures.

As of this printing the U.S. Coast Guard and Cape Hatteras National Seashore are still negotiating the possible transfer of title of this, the oldest lighthouse on the Outer Banks of North Carolina.

ELLEN FULCHER CLOUD
DECEMBER, 1992

Ocracoke Lighthouse as it is today.

APPENDIX A

Letters concerning the transfer of Ocracoke Lighthouse to Cape Hatteras National Seashore Park

Letter to Ellen F. Cloud from Mr. Floyd J. Lupton, administrative assistant, to Congressman Walter B. Jones April 27, 1990.

Letter to Ellen F. Cloud from Mr. Floyd J. Lupton, administrative assistant, to Congressman Walter B. Jones May 7, 1990.

Letter to Congressman Walter B. Jones from acting commandant of U.S. Coast Guard, May 10, 1990.

Letter to Ellen F. Cloud from Congressman Walter B. Jones, May 16, 1990.

Letter to regional director, Southeast Region, United States Department of the Interior, from Mr. Thomas Hartman, superintendent, Cape Hatteras National Seashore, May 31, 1990.

WALTER B. JONES
1st District, North Carolina

Telephone: Code 202: 225-3101

FLOYD J. LUPTON
Administrative Assistant

Committees:
Agriculture
Merchant Marine
and Fisheries

Congress of the United States
House of Representatives
Washington, DC 20515

April 27, 1990

Ms. Ellen F. Cloud
Ocracoke, NC 27960

Dear Ellen:

May I take this opportunity to express to you my warm and sincere appreciation for the beautiful hand painted pictures of the Ocracoke Lighthouse constructed in 1823 and also for the replica of the Ocracoke Lighthouse.

These pictures mean so very much to me and especially the fact that you painted them enhances their value even more. We have a very special place in our home for the lighthouse, and we cordially invite you to visit with us in Belhaven whenever you are passing that way.

Over a period of time, it has been a real pleasure for me to assist you in all matters relating to the lighthouse, and I commend you on your dedicated efforts to maintain this structure in its original state. We will continue to remain active in this matter until such time as a generator has been installed, the lights taken from the guardrail and the windows are constructed and installed. Already a letter has been written to Admiral Yost, Commandant, US Coast Guard regarding the transfer of the Lighthouse structure from the Coast Guard to the National Park Service. I am informed that such a request was made about six months ago and is currently pending in the New York office of the Coast Guard. Please be assured of our continued interest in this or any other matter of mutual concern to you and the good citizens of Ocracoke and at such time as a response has been received from Admiral Yost regarding this transfer, you will be promptly advised.

With warm personal regards and best wishes, I am

Sincerely,

Floyd

Floyd J. Lupton
Administrative Assistant

FJL:Lbo

WALTER B. JONES
[illegible] District, North Carolina
Phone: [illegible]

FLOYD J. LUPTON
[illegible]
[illegible]
AGRICULTURE
MERCHANT MARINE
AND FISHERIES

Congress of the United States
House of Representatives
Washington, DC 20515

May 7, 1990

Ms. Ellen F. Cloud
Ocracoke, NC 27960

Dear Ellen:

During your recent visit to Washington, we discussed the Ocracoke Lighthouse and what appears to be the Coast Guard delay in the installation of the generator to supply power to the lighthouse and also the installation of the proper windows.

I have on this date discussed these two issues directly with Captain Parks, Director, Aids to Navigation 5th Coast Guard District in Portsmouth, VA. He later advised me that the generator system would be completely installed with appropriate wiring to the navigation light and the lights removed from the outside rail by the end of May 1990.

Regarding the windows, Captain Parks advised that the windows were being milled by the Williams Port Preservation Trading Center under the supervision of the National Park Service and would be completed and installed during the coming summer.

As of this date, we have not received a response to our letter directed to Admiral Paul Yost, Commandant, US Coast Guard, regarding the transfer of the lighthouse structure to the National Park Service. However, at such time as a response has been received, you will be promptly advised.

With warm personal regards and best wishes, I am

Sincerely,

Floyd

Floyd J. Lupton
Administrative Assistant

FJL:Lbo

U.S. Department of Transportation

United States Coast Guard

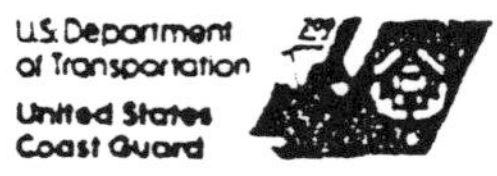

Commandant
United States Coast Guard

Washington, DC
Staff Symbol: (G-CC/104)
Phone: (202) 366-4280

5730

MAY 10 1990

The Honorable Walter B. Jones
Chairman, Committee on Merchant Marine
and Fisheries
House of Representatives
Washington, DC 20515

Dear Mr. Chairman:

This is in response to your letter of April 27, 1990, regarding Ocracoke Island Lighthouse, and a proposal to transfer the structure to the National Park Service.

We support transferring historic light stations located on (or adjacent to) National Park properties to the National Park Service. The National Park Service has asked us, however, to undertake these transfers on a case by case basis. This allows the appropriate Park Service unit to properly plan and budget for the increased maintenance responsibility which they incur when they assume ownership of the properties. As you are aware, Cape Hatteras Lighthouse, which has an active Coast Guard light, is owned by the National Park Service.

Possible transfer of Ocracoke Lighthouse to the National Park Service has been discussed with Park Service staff at the Cape Hatteras National Seashore, but we have not yet received a formal request for this action. We intend to pursue the transfer, and believe the Park Service is the best agency to ensure continued protection of historic Ocracoke Light.

Sincerely,

CLYDE T. LUSK, JR.
Vice Admiral, U.S. Coast Guard
Acting Commandant

WALTER B. JONES
1st District, North Carolina

Telephone Code 202: [illegible]

FLOYD J. LUPTO[illegible]
Administrative Assistant

Committees:
Agriculture
Merchant Marine
and Fisheries

Congress of the United States
House of Representatives
Washington, DC 20515

May 16, 1990

Ms. Ellen F. Cloud
Ocracoke, NC 27960

Dear Ellen:

During your visit to Washington in late April, you discussed with Floyd the possible transfer of the Ocracoke Island Lighthouse structure to the National Park Service. Immediately following your visit, a request was made directly to Admiral Paul A. Yost, Jr., Commandant, US Coast Guard with a request that this action be taken.

I am attaching a copy of a letter received on this date from the Acting Commandant which is self-explanatory. Even though the Park Service has discussed the possible transfer of the Ocracoke Lighthouse from the Coast Guard to the Park Service, the Coast Guard has not yet received a formal request for this action. You will also note that the Coast Guard intends to pursue the transfer and believes that the National Park Service is the best agency to ensure continued protection of this historic structure. May I suggest that you discuss this matter with Mr. Thomas Hartman, Superintendent, Cape Hatteras National Seashore in an effort to ascertain whether or not an official request for transfer has been made as of this date.

Please be assured of my continued personal interest in this transfer or any other matter of mutual interest to you personally and to the good citizens of Ocracoke.

With warm personal regards and best wishes, I am

Sincerely,

Walt

WALTER B. JONES
Member of Congress

WBJ:boL
Attachment

IN REPLY REFER TO:

UNITED STATES
DEPARTMENT OF THE INTERIOR
NATIONAL PARK SERVICE

Fort Raleigh National Historic Site Wright Brothers National Memorial
Cape Hatteras National Seashore
Route 1, Box 675
Manteo, North Carolina 27954-2708

H30
CAHA

May 31, 1990

Memorandum

To: Regional Director, Southeast Region

From: Superintendent, Cape Hatteras Group

Subject: Transfer of Ocracoke Lighthouse to National Park Service

The United States Coast Guard has expressed their interest in transferring the Ocracoke Lighthouse to the National Park Service. I believe this transfer would be in the best interests of the Service for several reasons:

The transfer would expand the park's opportunity to provide interpretation at this lighthouse, which is the second oldest active lighthouse in the United States.

The park has been performing significant maintenance on the structure for the past two years under Bicentennial Lighthouse program grants. Our park staff includes a Cultural Resource Management Specialist and an Exhibit Specialist, and we are therefore able to provide professional assistance as well as support staff for continuing maintenance.

The park houses two required occupants under a Special Use Permit in the Coast Guard's Lighthouse Keepers Quarters adjacent to the lighthouse. These employees provide security for the lighthouse.

The local village residents have formed the Ocracoke Preservation Society as an active organization dedicated to historic preservation on the island. They are very interested in proper preservation of the lighthouse and have been working closely with the park on this and other area projects.

With your approval, we shall advise the Coast Guard of our support for the transfer and ensure that all necessary review is conducted.

Thomas L. Hartman

Appendix B

Records of the Commissioner of the Revenue in the Department of the Treasury relating to the construction of Ocracoke Lighthouse.

An act supplementary to the act for the establishment and support of lighthouses, beacons, buoys, and public piers, March 2, 1793.

Report of Commissioner of Revenue, Tench Coxe, January 27, 1794.

Lighthouse on the Coast of North Carolina, communicated to the Senate, February 22, 1794.

Estimate of the cost of building a lighted beacon.

Report of Commissioner of Revenue, Tench Coxe, March 15, 1794.

Petition of Pilots of Ocracoke Bar, masters of vessels, merchants, owners of vessels, trading in and out of Ocracoke Inlet.

Lighthouses on the Coast of North Carolina, communicated to the House of Representatives, March 17, 1794.

Lighthouses on the Coast of North Carolina, communicated to the House of Representatives, April 15, 1794.

An Act to erect a Lighthouse on the headland of Cape Hatteras; and a lighted Beacon on Shell Castle Island in the harbor of Occacock in the state of North Carolina.

CHAP. XXVII.—*An Act supplementary to the act for the establishment and support of lighthouses, beacons, buoys, and public piers.*

SECTION 1. *Be it enacted by the Senate and House of Representatives of the United States of America in Congress assembled,* That all expenses, which shall accrue from the first day of July next inclusively, for the necessary support, maintenance and repairs of all lighthouses, beacons, buoys, the stakeage of channels on the sea-coast, and public piers, shall continue to be defrayed by the United States, until the first day of July, in the year one thousand seven hundred and ninety-four, notwithstanding such lighthouses, beacons, or public piers, with the lands and tenements thereunto belonging, and the jurisdiction of the same shall not, in the mean time, be ceded to, or vested in the United States, by the state or states respectively, in which the same may be; and that the said time be further allowed to the states respectively, to make such cession.

SEC. 2. *And be it further enacted,* That the Secretary of the Treasury be authorized and directed to cause a floating beacon or buoy to be provided and placed on Smith's Point shoal, in the Chesapeak bay, and a beacon or floating buoy at the southwest straddle on the Royal shoal, near Ocracoke inlet, in North Carolina.

APPROVED, March 2, 1793.

TREASURY DEPARTMENT, *Revenue Office, January 27, 1794.*

SIR:

I have the honor to communicate to you, the result of the inquiry into "the expediency of erecting a light-house on Occracock island, or elsewhere near the entrance of Occracock inlet, and an estimate of the probable expense," pursuant to the order of the Senate of the 28th of March, 1792.

The necessary examinations were directed to be made, in North Carolina, in time to have produced the information on which a report could have been transmitted to the Senate, in the session subsequent to that in which their order was made. But the difficulty of procuring a competent inspector, is represented as the cause of the delay, until June last; and the sickness and death of the collector of Edenton, who had been empowered to procure an inspector, increased the impediments.

Two ideas prevail upon the subject of a new light on that part of the sea coast. *First*, that a small wooden light-house or beacon, should be erected upon the land ceded by the State of North Carolina for the site of a light-house, which, it is supposed, could be effected for the sum of one thousand five hundred dollars, per estimate A; and, *Secondly*, that a stone light-house, of the first rate, should rather be erected upon the head land, or Cape of Hatteras, which, considering former precedents, and the enhanced rates of wages and materials, would probably cost twenty thousand dollars.

The inducements which occur in favor of erecting the smaller light-house, first mentioned, are, that it is the position which was indicated by the Legislature of the State, and by the traders of the vicinity; that it will be useful to vessels which make Occracock inlet late in the afternoon, or in the night, and that it can be effected at the least expense of the two buildings, towards which the inquiry necessarily turns.

The inducements to the erection of the larger light-house, are, 1st. The peculiarly dangerous nature of the navigation on that coast, by reason of the numerous shoals, and the frequency and suddenness of gales and tempests. 2d. The accommodation it will afford to the vessels which are bound to the several inlets of Pampticoe and Albemarle sounds, including that of Occracock. 3d. The accommodation to the numerous rich and increasing coasters, which ply between the States lying north and those lying south of Hatteras; and, lastly, to the numerous vessels trading with the European settlements in the West India islands, and on the American continent, to the southward of our territory, and to those employed in the transatlantic trade of the Southern States.

The traders of North Carolina, so far as could be ascertained, prefer at this time the erection of the light-house on Cape Hatteras. It is therefore probable, that it would appear most expedient to the State, were a comparison to be made; and it may be observed, that, in appropriating the national funds, Congress will, of course, have occasion to consider, in connection with local circumstances, those which apply to the accommodation and security of the national commerce. To these considerations the Legislature of North Carolina could not have been particularly led in making an appropriation of their own funds.

Particular attention was directed to the nature of the ground on which either light-house would be erected, in case the Legislature should determine to authorize the building. It appears that both situations afford very good foundations, without the least appearance of quicksands.

In regard to *the general expediency* of erecting a light-house in some part of the scene contemplated in the order of the Senate, the affirmative opinion is supported by the reasons already suggested in the two paragraphs of the preceding comparison. To those it may be added, that a profitable despatch in time of peace, and safety in time of war, will be promoted by the establishment of light-houses on the shoaly parts of our sea coast, as the vessels of the United States will be led thereby to navigate through and across the shoals without sailing round them, when expedition prompts, or hostile cruisers of greater draughts of water impel to those courses. An intimate knowledge of the shoals and banks on the eastern coasts, frequently protected unarmed vessels and those of small force from ships of greater size and strength, during the late war.

I have the honor to be, with great respect, sir, your most obedient servant,

TENCH COXE, *Commissioner of the Revenue.*

The SECRETARY OF THE TREASURY.

3d Congress.] **No. 20.** [1st Session.

LIGHT-HOUSE ON THE COAST OF NORTH CAROLINA.

COMMUNICATED TO THE SENATE, FEBRUARY 22, 1794.

The Secretary of the Treasury, pursuant to the order of the Senate of the 28th of March, 1792, "directing the Secretary of the Treasury to inquire into and report to Congress at their next session, the expediency of erecting a light-house on Occracock island, or elsewhere, near the entrance of Occracock inlet, and an estimate of the probable expense," respectfully makes the following report:

Upon receipt of that order, he instructed the Commissioner of the revenue, (who is charged with the immediate care of that branch of the treasury business, which respects light-house establishments,) to make the proper inquiries concerning the subject of it. But, having for a long time entertained an opinion that a light-house on some part of Cape Hatteras, would be an establishment of very general utility to the navigation of the United States, he judged it a fit occasion to unite with an examination of the scene indicated by the order, an examination of the situations on the Cape adapted to a light-house, and of such other circumstances as were necessary to be attended to, in forming a judgment of the practicability and expediency of erecting and maintaining a light-house on the Cape. And accordingly he charged the commissioner with the collateral inquiry likewise.

The result of the investigation on both points, is herewith presented in a letter from the commissioner, dated the 27th of January last, accompanied with an estimate of the expense of such an erection as appears eligible within the scene designated by the order.

It is submitted as the opinion of the Secretary, that it would be advisable as well to erect a light-house, of the first rate, on Cape Hatteras, (the requisite cession being previously obtained for the purpose) as to establish a beacon of the kind described in the estimate on the land ceded by the State of North Carolina, for the site of a light-house.

All which is respectfully submitted.

ALEXANDER HAMILTON, *Secretary of the Treasury.*

Treasury Department, *February* 20, 1794.

Estimate of the cost of building a lighted beacon, &c.

The building to be a wooden frame, fifty feet high, exclusively of the lanthorn. To contain one large lamp, with four wicks; to be twenty feet at the base, and to be reduced gradually to twelve feet at the top. It is thought necessary to continue the size of the building to that width at top, as it will be of great use as a sailing mark by day, and the larger the column the farther it may be visible.

Ranging timber, in board measure,		5,500 feet,
Scantling for framing in do.		2,500 feet,
Boards for floors and ceiling, &c.		2,800 feet,
Ditto for step ladders,		360 feet,
75 joists, board measure,		3,500 feet,
Waste of wooden materials,		1,000 feet,
		15,660 feet, at 16 dollars.
Including the charges of delivery at Occracock,		£93 19 2
Cedar to frame the windows and lanthorn,		10 00 0
Nails, spikes, bolts, locks, and hinges,		12 10 0
The lamp, and chains for it,		2 10 0
Glass for the lanthorn,		7 10 0
Ditto for the windows,		3 00 0
Workmanship, including the lanthorn, if of wood,		150 00 0
Painting three times,		20 00 0
If the lanthorn is made of iron and covered, &c. with copper, it would cost	£150	
Out of which might be deducted for one of wood,	40	
Leaves,		110 00 0
		£409 09 2
A house for the keeper, with a receptacle for oil, $400,		150 00 0
Total, $1,491 89, equal in Pennsylvania currency, to		£559 09 2

A.

Treasury Department, *Revenue Office, March 15th*, 1794.

Sir:

Having duly examined the object of the petition of the merchants, masters of vessels, and pilots of North Carolina, referred to you on the 20th instant by the House of Representatives, I have the honor to state to you what has occurred thereon.

It does not appear from the report of the Inspector of the proposed site on Occracock island, that he extended his view to the shell banks, or islands which lie one or two miles within Pampticoe Sound; but that he confined himself to a comparison of the several advantages which might be expected from light-houses, on some part of the chain of sand banks, or islands, which bound the ocean from Cape Hatteras to Cape Look-out. No immediate illustration of the object of the petition can, therefore, be obtained from the Inspector's report. It is worthy of observation, however, on account of the first consideration suggested by the petitioners, that the Inspector has represented "that no vessel could venture over the bar, or the swash, *in the night*, if there was a light-house erected near the inlet." But, it has been suggested, that a light on Shell Castle island, will be of use in enabling vessels, which shall have arrived at that place, to pursue their inward course to a more safe anchorage.

It is found, on examination, that the position desired by the petitioners, was contemplated by a principal informant in the course of the inquiry directed by the Senate, and that a comparison of the two sites, now under consideration, was communicated by him, favoring, in the first instance, the interior island, but, nevertheless, ultimately preferring the site on Occracock, because the island within was not then supposed to afford a safe foundation. There is, however, reason to believe, that a lighted beacon, like that contemplated in the bill of the Senate, may be safely erected on Shell Castle island.

It does not appear advisable, that the greater facility of defence should incline to a preference of any position, if otherwise less conducive to the proper uses of a light-house—*the warning* and *the direction* of navigators.

In a matter so perfectly local, it ought to be particularly remembered, that the original proceedings of the Legislature of North Carolina, pointed out the position on Occracock island, without giving an extension which might admit of building on any of the interior islands; and it appears, from the Inspector's report, that, during his examination at Occracock island, he consulted the pilots who reside on the spot, upon local points. Whether the present question ever arose in their conferences, is unknown at the treasury.

The resolution of the Senate directing the inquiry, was in terms fully comprehending all the contemplated situations; and it was communicated in September, 1792, to all the Collectors of the Customs, on the waters of Pampticoe and Albemarle sounds, in order to give due notoriety to a matter obviously liable to injury from local causes. The report of the Inspector was not made until June, 1793, and remains uncontradicted by the Collector, who transmitted it: nor has any different result to their inquiries been transmitted by the other Collectors.

Since the late reference to you, the ordinary use has been made of the nautical knowledge and experience of the superintendent of the Delaware establishments, and of his local knowledge. He does not coincide in opinion with the petitioners.

The minute and accurate local knowledge requisite to the formation of a decided opinion, entirely satisfactory to the mind, is not attainable. It appears, however, indubitable, that a lighted beacon, of the limited value contemplated, on either Occracock island, or Shell Castle island, will be greatly beneficial to the trade and navigation of North Carolina.

I have the honor to be, with great respect, sir, your most obedient servant,

TENCH COXE, *Commissioner of the Revenue.*

The Secretary of the Treasury.

To the Honorable the Congress of the United States, the representation of the subscribers, pilots, of Occracock bar, masters of vessels and merchants, owners of vessels, trading in and out at the same, showeth:

That they have understood there was a light-house about to be built contiguous to Occracock bar. And that they have further understood, that a survey has been made of the harbor and a report made in favor of Occracock island, as the place most proper to erect the light on. And as they have good reason to believe the light is intended to be erected for the benefit of vessels bound into or out of Occracock, they beg leave to state the reasons why they think the light-house should be erected on an island which stands in the harbor of Occracock, called Shell Castle, in preference of Occracock island.

1st. Because it will be a good mark for vessels to come in over the bar, by night or by day, which, at Occracock, it will not, and can only serve to inform when opposite the bar.

2d. Because it will be a good mark for vessels to run round the buoy, atthe southwest point of the Royal shoal, of a dark night, into safe anchorage, which would not be the case if at Occracock, as the distance from the Royal shoal to Occracock is too great to trust to any bearing to go into so narrow a channel.

3d. Because the materials for building the house can be cheaper landed at the Castle than any other place.

4th. Because it will be a better mark to cross the Bluff shoal in the night, than if it stood at Occracock, on account of its being much nearer and more ahead. And they beg leave further to add, that a light-house at Occracock will not have a single advantage over that of the Castle, the foundation being equally good.

5th. Because if, at any future period, it should be thought expedient to erect a fort for the protection of vessels at Occracock, the place which we now recommend for the light-house, is the only spot where a fort can be erected effectually to protect the shipping.

RICHARD WADE, *and fifty-six others.*

3d CONGRESS. | No. 21. | [1st SESSION.

LIGHT-HOUSE ON THE COAST OF NORTH CAROLINA.

COMMUNICATED TO THE HOUSE OF REPRESENTATIVES, MARCH 17, 1794.

The Secretary of the Treasury, to whom was referred the representation of Richard Wade and others, respectfully reports thereupon, as follows:

The paper A, herewith transmitted, (being a letter from the Commissioner of the revenue, who is charged with the immediate superintendence of the light-house establishments) exhibits the result of the investigation which has been made in relation to the matter in question.

There has not hitherto been discovered sufficient ground for preferring the place advocated by the representation, to that which was before contemplated, namely: the site on Occracock. But the opportunities for the future investigation have not been such as to authorize a definitive judgment. It has, however been thought advisable to expedite this report, as it is understood that a bill from the Senate is pending before the House which may involve a comparison of the two points.

Respectfully submitted.

ALEXANDER HAMILTON, *Secretary of the Treasury.*

TREASURY DEPARTMENT, *March 17th*, 1794.

3d CONGRESS. No. 23. [1st SESSION.

LIGHT HOUSE ON THE COAST OF NORTH CAROLINA.

COMMUNICATED TO THE HOUSE OF REPRESENTATIVES, APRIL 15, 1794.

Mr. BLOUNT, from the committee to whom was referred a bill, sent from the Senate, entitled "An act to erect a Light House on the head land of Cape Hatteras, and a lighted Beacon on Ocracock Island, in the State of North Carolina," together with the representation of Richard Wade, and others, and the report of the Secretary of the Treasury thereon, reported:

That, for the reasons stated in the representation of Richard Wade, and others, which are said, by a gentleman who has been upwards of twenty years acquainted with the navigation of Ocracock Inlet, to be just, your committee are of opinion that the lighted Beacon proposed to be erected on Ocracock Island, ought to be erected on an Island in the harbor of Ocracock, called Shell Castle; but, as that Island is situate nearly a league within the bar, they think it would be proper to make the beacon five feet higher than has been proposed, and two feet broader at the base; and, therefore, they recommend the following amendments to the bill, viz:

Strike out, in the third and fourth lines of the second section, the words "certain land ceded to the United States by the State of North Carolina, aforesaid, situate on Ocracock Island, in said State," and insert, instead thereof, the words, "an island in the harbor of Ocracock, called Shel' Castle." Insert, in the fifth line of the second section, after the word "fifty," the word five; and, in the same line, after the word "twenty," the word two.

CHAP. XXVIII.—*An Act to erect a Lighthouse on the headland of Cape Hatteras; and a lighted Beacon on Shell Castle Island in the harbor of Occacock in the state of North Carolina.*

SECTION 1. *Be it enacted by the Senate and House of Representatives of the United States of America in Congress assembled,* That as soon as the jurisdiction of so much of the head-land of Cape Hatteras in the state of North Carolina, as the President of the United States shall deem sufficient and most proper for the convenience and accommodation of a lighthouse shall have been ceded to the United States, it shall be the duty of the Secretary of the Treasury to provide by contract which shall be approved by the President of the United States, for building a lighthouse thereon of the first rate, and furnishing the same with all necessary supplies, and also to agree for the salaries or wages of the person or persons who may be appointed by the President for the superintendence and care of building said lighthouse: And the President is hereby authorized to make said appointments. That the number and disposition of the lights in the said lighthouse shall be such, as may tend to distinguish it from others, and as far as practicable, to prevent mistakes in navigators.

SEC. 2. *And be it further enacted,* That the Secretary of the Treasury be authorized to provide by contract, which shall be approved by the President of the United States, for building on an island in the harbor of Occacock, called Shell Castle, a lighted beacon of a wooden frame fifty-five feet high, to be twenty-two feet at the base, and to be reduced gradually to twelve feet at the top exclusively of the lantern, which shall be made to contain one large lamp with four wicks, and for furnishing the same with all necessary supplies. *Provided,* That no such lighted beacon shall be erected, until a cession of a sufficient quantity of land on the said island shall be made to the United States by the consent of the legislature of the state of North Carolina.

SEC. 3. *And be it further enacted,* That sufficient monies be appropriated for the erecting and completing the buildings aforesaid out of any monies heretofore appropriated which may remain unexpended, after satisfying the purposes for which they were appropriated, or out of any monies which may be in the treasury not subject to any prior appropriation.

APPROVED, May 13, 1794.

End Notes

1. *The Republican*, March 18,1839 (newspaper at Washington, N.C.).

2. *Carteret County During the American Revolution* (A Bicentennial Project of the Carteret County Bicentennial Commission)

3. Carteret County Register of Deeds, Beaufort, N.C.

4. David Stick, *Outer Banks of North Carolina* (Chapel Hill: The University of North Carolina Press, 1958), pp. 302-203.

5. *Ibid.*

6. *Ibid.*

7. *Ibid.*

8. David Stick, *The North Carolina Lighthouses* (Raleigh Division of Archives and History, North Carolina Department of Cultural Resources).

9. Blount Papers, Raleigh, Division of Archives and History, North Carolina Department of Cultural Resources.

10. Records of The Bureau of Lighthouses and its Predecessors 1789-1939, Department of Transportation, Record Group 26, National Archives of the United States.

11. Records in the custody of the Commissioner of the Revenue, in the Department of the Treasury.

12. Microfilm #1373—Lighthouse Keepers, National Archives of the United States.

13. *Ibid.*

14. *Ibid.*

15. *Ibid.*

16. Lightkeeper's logbook, Ocracoke Station, Record Group 26, National Archives of the United States.

17. *Ibid.*

18. *Ibid.*

19. *Ibid.*

20. Pamtico was a common spelling for Pamlico in most records in the 1700s and early 1800s.

21. *Ibid.*

22. Microfilm, Lightkeepers.

Photo and Illustration Credits

Front Cover	Photo by Paulette Chitwood.
Page xiv	Photo: Courtesy of the Outer Banks History Center, Manteo, N.C. From the Aycock Brown Collection.
Page xv	Map: Courtesy of the Library of Congress, Washington.
Pages 12 & 13	Photos: Prints Courtesy of Outer Banks History Center, Manteo, N.C. Originals: National Archives & Records Administration; Washington D.C.
Page 14	Plat: Records of the United States Coast Guard; General Services Administration; National Archives and Records Administration, Washington D.C.
Page 18	Photo: Courtesy of Ward Garrish
Page 19	Photo: Courtesy of Gaynelle Spencer Tillett
Page 20	Photo: Courtesy of Gaynelle Spencer Tillett
Page 22	Photo: Courtesy of the Outer Banks History Center, Maneo NC. From the Aycock Brown Collection.
Page 47	Photos: By Sally Newell
Page 48	Photo: By Sally Newell
Page 51	Illustration: Original Artwork by Butsie Brown

Glossary of Terms

Bar a sand bar in the inlet that prevents vessels from passing

Master a captain of a ship

Muntins a frame for holding the glass panes of a window

Needling the act of using a sharp object to clean a valve which controls the flow of oil to a wick

Lightering the act of taking part or all of the cargo off a ship and into smaller boats to make it lighter in the water, enabling the ship to cross sand bars in the inlet

Tender a small boat for carrying passengers and supplies to or from larger ships or lighthouses

Windjammer a sail ship

INDEX